WELCOME TO THE FARM

Cotton Picker

Samantha Bell

Published in the United States of America
by Cherry Lake Publishing
Ann Arbor, Michigan
www.cherrylakepublishing.com

Content Adviser: Gary Powell, Weed Science Research Technician, Michigan State University
Reading Adviser: Marla Conn MS, Ed., Literacy specialist, Read-Ability, Inc.
Photo Credits: © Jim Parkin/Shutterstock, cover, 1, 2; © Carol M. Highsmith/Library of Congress, 4; © Lindasj22/Shutterstock, 6, 12, 14; © Rob Byron/Shutterstock, 8; © VanHart/Shutterstock, 10; © IrinaK/Shutterstock, 16; © zhengzaishuru/Shutterstock, 18; © liza1979/Shutterstock, 20

Library of Congress Cataloging-in-Publication Data
Names: Bell, Samantha, author. | Bell, Samantha. Welcome to the farm.
Title: Cotton picker / Samantha Bell.
Description: Ann Arbor : Cherry Lake Publishing, [2016] | Series: Welcome to the farm | Includes bibliographical references and index.
Identifiers: LCCN 2015047226| ISBN 9781634710350 (hardcover) | ISBN 9781634711340 (pdf) | ISBN 9781634712330 (pbk.) | ISBN 9781634713320 (ebook)
Subjects: LCSH: Cotton-picking machinery—Juvenile literature.
Classification: LCC S715.C64 B44 2016 | DDC 633.5/1—dc23
LC record available at http://lccn.loc.gov/2015047226

Cherry Lake Publishing would like to acknowledge the work of the Partnership for 21st Century Skills. Please visit www.p21.org for more information.

Printed in the United States of America
Corporate Graphics

Table of Contents

What things do plants need to grow?

Ready to Pick

Cotton plants have been growing all summer. Now they are ready to be picked. Some farmers use a cotton picker.

This machine has heads on the front. They pick the **bolls**.

Spindles

Inside the heads are **spindles**. They turn. They pull the **fibers** from the bolls.

Collecting the Fibers

A **doffer** grabs the fibers. It takes them off the spindles. It works like a comb.

The fibers move into a big basket. Soon the basket is full.

DO NOT EXCEED
ENGINE 1300 R.P.M.
WARNING
OPERATE POSITION (TAMPER LOCKED)
HOLD TAMPER LEVER IN DOWN POSITION
UNTIL TAMPER CYLINDER PLATE IS LOCKED

The cotton fibers go in a boll **buggy**.

Ready to Use

The cotton is rolled into a **bale**. A truck takes it to a **gin**.

How does cotton feel to touch?

The cotton is cleaned. It is ready to use.

Cotton is used to make many things, like clothes. All thanks to a cotton picker!

Find Out More

Nelson, Robin. *From Cotton to T-Shirt*. Minneapolis: Lerner Publications, 2013.

Cotton Australia—How Do We Pick Cotton?
http://cottonaustralia.com.au/blog/article/how-do-we-pick-cotton-version-2-baler-pickers
Watch a video showing how cotton pickers work.

Glossary

bale (BALE) a large bundle of goods tied tightly together
bolls (BOHLZ) the cases around the seeds of plants
buggy (BUHG-ee) a cart or truck used to move heavy things
doffer (DOHF-er) the part of a cotton picker that grabs the fibers
fibers (FYE-burz) long threads
gin (JIN) a machine that separates seeds and dirt from cotton fibers
spindles (SPIN-duhlz) the round sticks or rods on a spinning wheel that hold and wind thread

Home and School Connection

Use this list of words from the book to help your child become a better reader. Word games and writing activities can help beginning readers reinforce literacy skills.

a
all
are
bale
basket
be
been
big
boll
bolls
buggy
cleaned
clothes
collecting
comb
cotton
do
does
doffer
farmers
feel
fibers
from
front
full
gin
grabs
grow
growing
has
have
heads
how
inside
into
it
like
machine
many
move
need
now
off
on
pick
picked
picker
plants
pull
ready
rolled
some
soon
spindles
summer
takes
thanks
the
them
they
things
this
to
touch
truck
turn
use
what
works

Index

About the Author

Samantha Bell is a children's book writer, illustrator, teacher, and mom of four busy kids. Her articles, short stories, and poems have been published online and in print.